# Fall Classics

*2023* ↑ (handwritten annotation above title)

*find a good veggie recipe Love Mom J.* (handwritten note)

Autumn Vegetarian Casseroles

BY

Julia Chiles

Copyright 2020 - Julia Chiles

# License Notes

No part of this Book can be reproduced in any form or by any means including print, electronic, scanning or photocopying unless prior permission is granted by the author.

All ideas, suggestions and guidelines mentioned here are written for informative purposes. While the author has taken every possible step to ensure accuracy, all readers are advised to follow information at their own risk. The author cannot be held responsible for personal and/or commercial damages in case of misinterpreting and misunderstanding any part of this Book

# Thanks for Purchasing My Book! - Here's Your Reward!

Thank you so much for purchasing my book! As a reward for your purchase, you can now receive free books sent to you every week. All you have to do is just subscribe to the list by entering your email address in the box below and I will send you a notification every time I have a free promotion running. The books will absolutely be free with no work at all from you! Who doesn't want free books? No one! *There are free and discounted books every day*, and an email is sent to you 1-2 days beforehand to remind you so you don't miss out. It's that easy! Enter your email now to get started!

http://julia-chiles.subscribemenow.com

# Table of Contents

Introduction ............................................................................................................. 7

    5 Alarm 4 Bean Stew ...................................................................................... 8

    Sweet Potato Noodle Stir-Fry ....................................................................... 10

    Almond Stir-Fry ............................................................................................ 12

    Easy Cabbage Casserole ............................................................................... 14

    Plantain Mash Casserole .............................................................................. 16

    Guava Casserole ........................................................................................... 19

    Ramen Salad Casserole ................................................................................ 21

    Cinnamon-Sugar Tostones Casserole .......................................................... 23

    Eggplant and Tofu Casserole ....................................................................... 25

    Cheesy Italian Mushroom Casserole ........................................................... 27

    Medi Veggie Casserole ................................................................................ 29

    Basil, Avocado, and Onion Casserole ......................................................... 31

    Sesame Tofu Casserole ................................................................................ 33

    Sweet Honey Ginger Rice ............................................................................ 35

    Okra and Cucumbers ................................................................................... 37

Tofu & Bok Choy Casserole .................................................................................. 39

Mushroom Fajita Casserole .................................................................................. 41

Soba Noodle Taco Casserole ................................................................................ 43

Honey Ginger Penne ............................................................................................ 45

Onion and Herb Gravy Over Roasted Potato's ..................................................... 47

Spicy Tofu & Mushroom Casserole ...................................................................... 50

Chipotle Stir-Fry ................................................................................................... 52

Vegetarian Greek Pizza ........................................................................................ 54

BBQ Pizza Casserole ........................................................................................... 56

'Meaty' Vegetarian Chow Mein ............................................................................ 58

Cauliflower de Provence ...................................................................................... 60

Blackbean & Cucumber Casserole with Tzatziki ................................................. 62

Potatoes and Spirals Bake .................................................................................... 64

Greek Mushrooms and Stewed Tomatoes ............................................................ 66

Honey Garlic Potatoes & Peppers ........................................................................ 68

Baked Vegetarian Chili ........................................................................................ 71

Kale and Artichoke Linguine Casserole ............................................................... 73

Turmeric Casserole .............................................................................................. 75

Cucumber & Asparagus Casserole ...... 77

Shirataki Noodles ...... 79

Instant Pot Yogurt Casserole ...... 81

Sesame Noodle Casserole ...... 83

I.P Cantaloupe & Cucumber Bake ...... 85

Cauliflower Gnocchi Casserole ...... 87

Sriracha Thyme Casserole ...... 89

Cayenne Casserole ...... 91

Rice Noodle Bake ...... 93

Kale & Carrots Casserole ...... 95

Quick & Easy I.P Veggie Curry ...... 97

Sweet Vegetable Curry ...... 99

Spicy Cabbage Casserole ...... 101

Apple Pie French Toast Instant Pot Casserole ...... 103

Peppers with Mushrooms, Avocado and Eggs ...... 105

Eggplant & Pumpkin Puttanesca ...... 107

Author's Afterthoughts ...... 109

# Introduction

Need some meatless fall cheer? Fall Classics: 49 Autumn Vegetarian Casseroles is the right place to be! 50 unique autumn vegetarian casseroles for every palette and occasion!

**Note:**

*NPR - Natural Pressure Release*

*QPR - Quick Pressure Release*

# 5 Alarm 4 Bean Stew

Hot!! Makes 4 servings

**Ingredients:**

- 1 tbsp olive oil
- 1 can black beans, drained and washed
- 1 can garbanzo beans, drained and washed
- 1 can dark red kidney beans, washed and drained
- 1 can cannellini beans, washed and drained
- 1 tsp minced garlic
- 1/2 diced onion
- 2 diced jalapenos or green chilies
- 1 can veggie mix, drained and washed
- 5 spice powder
- 4 cup vegetable broth

**Directions:**

Preheat the oven to 350F and prepare 9x11 casserole dish.

Swirl oil around casserole dish.

In bowl, mix together black beans, garbanzo beans, kidney beans, cannellini beans, onions, veggies, 5 spice powder, vegetable broth.

Pour ingredients into an even layer and bake uncovered for 30 minutes.

# Sweet Potato Noodle Stir-Fry

Great lunch option! Makes 2 servings

**Ingredients:**

- ½ tbsp olive oil
- ½ onion, diced
- ½ tsp minced or grated garlic
- 1/2 cup garbanzo beans
- 2 cups worth sweet potato spirals
- ½ tablespoon crushed walnuts or silvered almonds
- 1/2 cup diced mushrooms
- 1/3 cup matchstick carrots
- ½ tablespoon diced thyme
- ½ tablespoon diced oregano
- ½ tsp lemon juice
- 1/4 cup water or chicken stock
- Shredded cheddar cheese for topping
- Chopped parsley for topping

**Directions:**

Heat pot on high

Pour in oil, onions, garlic and sauté 30-45 seconds swirling oils around.

Sauté beans, nuts, mushrooms, carrots, thyme, oregano, water 30-45 seconds.

Toss in sweet potato spirals.

Warm through, transfer to plate, top each with cheese and parsley.

# Almond Stir-Fry

Also great with ground turkey! Makes 1 serving

**Ingredients:**

- 2 tbsp olive oil
- 1/3 tsp rice vinegar
- ½ tsp sesame oil
- ½ tbsp diced onion
- ½ tsp minced garlic
- 1-2 drops chili oil
- 1/2-piece ginger chopped
- 1 tbsp slivered almonds
- ¼ cup worth edamame or snow peas
- 1/2 cup cooked jasmine rice
- ½ tsp vegetable bouillon paste (such as Better Then Bouillon vegetable flavor)

**Directions:**

Preheat oven to 350F and prepare 8x8 pan.

Warm skillet over high heat and toast almonds until fragrant then transfer to paper plate.

In small bowl, whisk together oil, vinegar, sesame oil, onion, garlic, chili oil, ginger, edamame, and bouillon.

Pour in skillet and stir fry 1 minute.

Pour in cooked rice and toss.

Top with almonds.

# Easy Cabbage Casserole

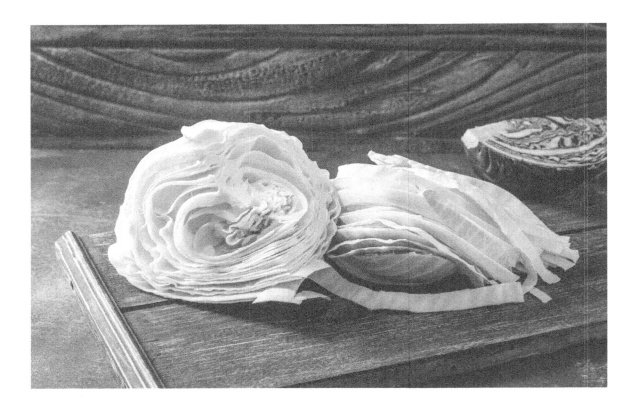

Let your imagination loose with this recipe! Makes 2 servings.

**Ingredients:**

- ½ tbsp olive oil
- 2/3 cup diced onion
- 2 crushed cloves of garlic
- 4 cups of chopped cabbage
- 1/4 cup toasted almond slivers
- ¼ tsp nutmeg
- 1/3 cup grated parmesan
- Olive oil for drizzling
- ½ cup water

**Directions:**

In skillet, warmed over medium heat and oil sauté cabbage, onions, garlic 45 seconds – 1 minute.

Add in almond slivers, nutmeg, water and bring to a boil.

Remove from heat.

Cover bottom of pan with cabbage, cheese, repeat.

Drizzle with olive oil.

Bake 25-30 minutes.

# Plantain Mash Casserole

You will love this dish! Makes 4 servings

**Ingredients:**

- ½ stick butter
- 1/2 diced onion
- 1 Tsp minced garlic
- ½ tbsp Adobo seasoning
- 1/3 cup worth chopped roasted red peppers
- 4-6 large plantains, mashed
- 1 Tsp diced tomatoes and green chiles, drained
- ½ tbsp chopped parsley
- ½ tbsp chopped cilantro
- ½ tsp capers
- 2-3 cups low sodium beef broth
- Parmesan cheese for topping

**Directions:**

Preheat oven to 350F and prepare 9x9 dish

Chop plantain and boil for approx. 20-30 minutes to soften.

Mash.

In pot, warmed over medium-high heat melt butter then sauté onion and garlic 30-45 seconds.

Remove from heat and stir in Adobo seasoning, roasted red peppers, mashed plantains, parsley, cilantro, capers, and broth.

Spread evenly into dish.

Top with cheese and bake 30 minutes.

# Guava Casserole

Awesome! Makes 4 servings

**Ingredients:**

- 1 package phyllo dough
- 1 cup guava paste
- 1 (8 oz.) block of cream cheese
- 3 egg whites for egg wash

**Directions:**

Preheat oven to 350F and prepare 9x9 or 8x8 pan.

Mix together paste and cream cheese.

Lay 2-4 pieces of dough in bottom of pan.

Top with even layer of Guava and cream cheese mixture.

Repeat.

Brush top pastry layers with egg wash.

Bake 30 minutes.

# Ramen Salad Casserole

Everyone will love this! Makes 4 servings

**Ingredients:**

- 1 tbsp olive oil
- 2 package ramen noodles (discard seasoning packet)
- 1/2 cup whole kernel corn
- 1/2 cup black beans
- 1/2 yellow bell pepper, julienned
- 1 diced habanero
- 2 cups red bell pepper and ginger broth

**Directions:**

Preheat oven to 350F, prepare 9x9 dish and wipe down with oil.

Mix together noodles, corn, black beans, bell pepper, habanero, broth.

# Cinnamon-Sugar Tostones Casserole

Great for brunch! Makes 4 servings.

**Ingredients:**

- 3-5 large plantains, sliced lengthwise
- 1 package phyllo dough
- ¼ cup Cinnamon-Sugar
- 1 (8 oz.) package cream cheese
- 1/3 cup egg wash or 3 egg whites

**Directions:**

Preheat oven to 350F and prepare 9x9 dish.

Mix together cinnamon sugar and cream cheese.

To soften plantains, boil 10-15 minutes.

Lay dough in bottom of pan.

Top with plantains, spread on cream cheese mixture evenly.

Top with dough then brush with egg wash.

Repeat.

Bake 30 minutes.

# Eggplant and Tofu Casserole

Try it with Greek seasoning. Makes 4 servings

**Ingredients:**

- 1 large eggplant, cut into 1-inch cubes
- 1 onion, cut into 1-inch pieces
- 2 cups quartered tomatoes
- 1 large red bell pepper, cut into 1-inch pieces
- 1 block firm cubed tofu, patted dry
- 1 teaspoon lemon zest
- ¼ cup olive oil
- 1 summer squash, cut into 1-inch pieces
- ½ cup water
- 1 cup shredded feta cheese

**Directions:**

Preheat to 350F and prepare a casserole dish.

In dish, mix together eggplant, bell pepper, squash, onion, tomatoes, tofu.

Toss with lemon zest and oil.

Sprinkle with cheese; bake 20-25 minutes.

# Cheesy Italian Mushroom Casserole

Delicious! Makes 4 servings.

**Ingredients:**

- 2-3 cups jasmine rice
- 2 cups baby cremini mushrooms, chopped and washed
- 1 teaspoon Italian seasoning
- ½ teaspoon ground pepper
- 3 tbsp plain breadcrumbs
- 2 tbsp grated parmesan cheese

**Directions:**

Preheat oven to 350F and prepare a 9x9 dish

Mix together rice, mushrooms, seasoning, pepper, breadcrumbs, cheese.

Bake 30 minutes.

# Medi Veggie Casserole

Sub ramen for the cabbage! Makes 4 servings.

**Ingredients:**

- 2 cups shredded cabbage
- 1/2 cup chickpeas, rinsed
- 1/2 sliced cucumber
- 1 small sliced tomato
- 1/3 cup diced olives
- ½ cup crumbled feta cheese
- 1 1/2 cups grapes
- 1 tablespoon lemon zest
- 4 tablespoons olive oil
- ½ cup water

**Directions:**

In a large bowl, toss together chickpeas, cucumber, tomato, olives, feta, turkey cubes, grapes, lemon zest, olive oil, water.

Bake 30 minutes.

# Basil, Avocado, and Onion Casserole

Great on flatbread too! Makes 1 serving

**Ingredients:**

- 1 avocado, diced
- 1 onion, diced
- 1/3 cup whole kernel corn
- 4-6 basil leaves, sliced
- 1 cup shredded mozzarella
- 2 package ramen noodles, discard seasoning packet
- Pepper to taste
- 1 cup water

**Directions:**

Preheat oven to 350F and prepare 9x9 dish.

In a large bowl, mix together avocado, onions, corn, basil, and sprinkle with cheese.

# Sesame Tofu Casserole

Cook this one pot meal in short stages; Makes 4 servings

**Ingredients:**

- 1/4 cup canola or veg. oil
- 1 tsp sesame oil
- 1/2 block cubed extra firm tofu
- ½ tsp ginger, ground
- 1/2 tsp white pepper
- ½ tsp diced thyme
- ½ tbsp diced parsley
- 1/3 cup white wine
- 1 cup worth shiitake mushrooms
- 1 cup worth diced broccoli
- 1/2 cup jasmine rice
- 2 cups chicken broth

**Directions:**

Warm Dutch oven over high heat.

Add oils and sauté tofu cubes approx. 2-3 minutes, stir in spices and herbs, pour in wine, stir, add mushrooms, broccoli, rice, and broth.

Bring to a boil, reduce heat, cover, simmer 20-25 minutes.

# Sweet Honey Ginger Rice

Add chia or sesame seeds! Makes 4 servings

**Ingredients:**

- 1 tbsp oil
- 1 tsp sesame oil
- 1 package stir fry vegetables
- 1/2 tsp turmeric
- 1 tsp ginger, minced or grated
- 2 tbsp soy sauce,
- ½ tbsp honey, brown sugar
- 1 cup pineapple juice
- 1/2 cup jasmine

**Directions:**

Warm Dutch oven over med - high heat.

Add oil, vegetables, turmeric, ginger, soy sauce, honey, brown sugar, pineapple juice, rice.

Bring to a boil, let simmer 20-30 minutes.

# Okra and Cucumbers

Great as a snack! Makes 4 servings

**Ingredients:**

- ½ tbsp olive oil
- 1 bag okra
- 2 sliced cucumbers
- 2 cloves garlic, grated
- 1/2 cup grated carrots
- 2 cups cauliflower rice
- 1/3 tsp sea salt
- 1/3 tsp onion powder
- ½ tsp pepper
- 1/3 tsp lemon peel
- ½ tsp Greek seasoning
- ¾ cup water

**Directions:**

In pot, combine olive oil, okra, cucumbers, garlic, carrots, cauliflower rice, sea salt, onion powder, pepper, lemon peel, Greek seasoning, water.

Cook on high 4 minutes

*NPR 1 MINUTE THEN QPR*

# Tofu & Bok Choy Casserole

Add in a burger crumble! Makes 4 servings

**Ingredients:**

- 2 tbsp veg. or canola oil
- ½ cup jasmine rice
- 1/2 block cubed firm tofu (pat dry)
- 2 cups worth of chopped bok choy
- 1 tbsp soy sauce
- 1/2 tbsp melted butter
- 1 tsp brown sugar
- 1/4 tsp pepper
- 1 tbsp white wine

**Directions:**

Warm Dutch oven over medium high heat.

Add oil, soy sauce, butter, brown sugar, pepper, wine.

Sauté tofu and bok choy 2-4 minutes.

Pour in wine, stir.

# Mushroom Fajita Casserole

Try using fresh herbs. Makes 2 servings

**Ingredients:**

- 2 cups diced white mushrooms
- 2 cloves garlic, chopped
- 1 cup lettuce, shredded
- 1 sliced tomato
- 1 sliced onion
- 1 tbsp olive oil
- ½ tbsp Dijon mustard
- 2/3 tsp chili powder
- 4 corn tortillas
- ½ cup shredded cheddar cheese

**Directions:**

Preheat oven to 350F and prepare 9x9 dish.

In a small bowl, whisk together olive oil, Dijon mustard, and chili powder.

Mix together diced mushrooms, diced garlic, shredded lettuce, tomato slices, onion slices.

Pour olive oil mixture over mushroom/lettuce.

Top with tortillas and cheese.

Bake 30 minutes.

# Soba Noodle Taco Casserole

Try using fresh herbs. Makes 2 servings

**Ingredients:**

- 2 cups worth soba noodles
- 2 cloves garlic, chopped
- 1 cup lettuce, shredded
- 1/3 cup diced button mushrooms
- 1 sliced tomato
- 1 sliced onion
- 1 tbsp diced black olives
- 1 tbsp olive oil
- ½ tbsp salsa
- 2/3 tsp chili powder
- ½ cup shredded cheddar cheese

**Directions:**

Preheat oven to 350F and prepare 9x9 dish.

Mix together soba noodles, diced garlic, shredded lettuce, tomato slices, onion slices, black olives, olive oil, salsa, chili powder, cheese.

Lay evenly in casserole dish.

Bake 30 minutes.

# Honey Ginger Penne

Delicious! Makes 2 servings

**Ingredients:**

- 1 tbsp olive oil (use coconut oil for a change of flavor)
- ½ tsp pepper
- 1/3 cup bell pepper, diced (optional)
- 1 tsp ginger, minced or grated
- 2 teaspoons organic honey
- 1 teaspoon walnuts
- 1 tbsp-1/4 cup spinach diced
- ½ tbsp diced parsley, diced
- 1/2 cup penne pasta, cooked al dente and drained- DO NOT RINSE
- 2 cups water

**Directions:**

In skillet, add oil, pepper, diced bell peppers, ginger, spinach, and walnuts. And sauté 25-30 seconds.

Toss in penne and water.

# Onion and Herb Gravy Over Roasted Potato's

Chia seed powder is chocked full of antioxidants, fiber, and omega-3''s. Makes 4-6 servings.

**Ingredients:**

- 15-20 small purple potatoes
- Olive oil for drizzling
- 2 diced shallots
- 1 teaspoon finely diced thyme
- 2 cups stock or water
- 1 teaspoon finely diced Italian oregano
- 2-3 tbsp chia seed powder
- ¼ cup breadcrumbs
- 2 tbsp parmesan cheese, grated

**Directions:**

Preheat oven to 400F and line baking 9x9 dish with aluminum foil.

Quarter cut potatoes lay in single layer on sheet and drizzle with olive oil.

Cover with clear wrap and let chill in fridge.

In a skillet, toast chia seed powder.

Then, whisk in stock/water, onions, chia seed powder.

Bring to a boil, cover, and reduce heat and simmer for 25-30 minutes or till reduced by half. Stir occasionally.

Stir in diced oregano, thyme, and rosemary.

Bring potatoes to room temp.

Cover with gravy and cheese.

Bake 35 minutes.

# Spicy Tofu & Mushroom Casserole

Too hot? Try paprika! Makes 2 servings.

**Ingredients:**

- ½ block firm, silken tofu
- 1 cup shiitake mushrooms, sliced
- 1 teaspoon ground ginger
- ½ cup worth edamame
- 2 stalks bok choy, chopped
- 1 teaspoon ground turmeric or paprika
- ¼ tsp five spice powder
- 1/3 tsp oregano
- 1/4 tsp rosemary
- 1/3 cups garbanzo beans, washed and drained
- 2-3 cups vegetable stock

**Directions:**

In pot, combine tofu, mushrooms, ginger, edamame, bok choy, turmeric, five spice powder, oregano, rosemary, beans, stock.

Cook on high 5 minutes.

*QPR*

# Chipotle Stir-Fry

Pomegranates have anti-inflammatory properties! Makes 2 servings.

**Ingredients:**

- ½ jasmine rice
- ½ tbsp olive oil or coconut oil
- ¼ cup walnuts
- ¼ cup julienned onions
- ¼ cup dried pomegranates
- 1/3 cup chopped chipotle peppers
- 1 meatless burger crumble
- 2 cups water

**Directions:**

In pot, combine rice, oil, walnuts, onions, cranberries/pomegranates, chipotle peppers, burger, water.

Sauté 1 minute.

Add in rice and stock.

Bring to boil, reduce heat, cover, let simmer 10-15 minutes.

# Vegetarian Greek Pizza

Excellent for brunch! Makes 1 pizza.

**Ingredients:**

- 1 crushed cauliflower pizza crust or 3-4 cups cauliflower rice
- ½ teaspoon Greek seasoning
- ½ tsp garlic, minced
- ¼ tsp onion grated or minced
- 2 tbsp diced black olives
- 1 red pepper, chopped- stems and seed removed
- 1 cup shredded feta

**Directions:**

Preheat oven to 350F and prepare 9x9 dish.

Place broken crust or rice in bottom of dish.

Mix together, add red pepper pieces, Italian seasoning, grated or minced onion, minced garlic, minced black olives.

Spread sauce on cauliflower crust and top with shredded cheese.

# BBQ Pizza Casserole

Love! Makes 1 pizza.

**Ingredients:**

- 1 broken cauliflower pizza crust or cauliflower rice
- ¼ teaspoon Italian seasoning
- 2-3 sweet red pepper, chopped- stems and seed removed
- ¼ tsp onion powder or julienned and caramelized
- ½ tsp garlic, minced
- ½-1/3 cup crumbled feta cheese
- 2/3 cup BBQ sauce

**Directions:**

Mix together BBQ sauce, Italian seasoning, onion powder and minced garlic.

Spread sauce on cauliflower crust and top with shredded chicken and cheese.

# 'Meaty' Vegetarian Chow Mein

Excellent meat for tacos! Makes approx. 4-6 cups.

**Ingredients:**

- 3 tsp olive oil or avocado oil
- ½ cup cauliflower florets
- 1/3 cup sliced shiitake mushrooms
- 1/2 teaspoon paprika
- 1/2 teaspoon sweet ginger
- 1/4 teaspoon garlic powder
- 1/3 teaspoon onion powder
- 1/3 teaspoon oregano
- ½ cup rice
- 1 can Chow Mein Vegetables

**Directions:**

Preheat 400F & lining 9x9 dish with aluminum foil.

Meanwhile mix smoked paprika, chili powder, garlic powder, onion powder, oregano.

Place cauliflower and sliced mushrooms in dish then top with chow mein vegetables.

Sprinkle with paprika mix.

Roast 18-22 minutes or until edges of cauliflower starts to turn at edges.

# Cauliflower de Provence

Try it with broccoli! Makes 2 servings

**Ingredients:**

- olive oil spray
- ½ tsp turmeric
- 1 teaspoon Herbs de Provence
- ½ teaspoon red pepper flakes
- 1/2 sweet onion, chopped
- 1 tsp garlic, minced
- 1 carrot, julienned
- 1 cup chopped kale
- 2 heads of cauliflower, cut into florets
- 1 cup garbanzo beans, washed and drained
- 4 cups low-sodium vegetable broth
- Feta cheese, crumbled
- Chopped parsley or Italian oregano

**Directions:**

Preheat oven to 425F and prepare 9x9 casserole dish

Mix together turmeric, Herbs de Provence, red pepper flakes, onion, garlic, carrot, kale, cauliflower, garbanzo beans, broth.

Cook on high pressure 7 minutes.

*QPR*

Transfer to plates and top with cheese and herbs.

# Blackbean & Cucumber Casserole with Tzatziki

Try various beans! Makes 4-6 servings

**Ingredients:**

- 1 cup black beans, washed and drained
- 2 long seedless cucumbers, sliced
- 1 can cream of celery soup
- 1/3 tsp black pepper
- 1 tbsp diced basil
- 2 cups cold plain Greek yogurt
- 3 ½ teaspoons minced garlic
- ⅓ cup chopped dill
- 1 Tbsp lemon juice
- Crumbled feta cheese or shredded mozzarella (optional

**Directions:**

Preheat oven to 350F and prepare 9x9 dish.

Puree yogurt, garlic, dill, lemon juice, black pepper in a blender or food processor; store in refrigerator.

Mix together black beans, cucumbers, condensed soup, basil.

Spread evenly into dish and top with sauce.

Bake 30 minutes.

# Potatoes and Spirals Bake

No Greek seasoning? Use Italian seasoning! Makes 2 servings

**Ingredients:**

- 2 cups diced potatoes
- 10 cherry tomatoes, halved
- 1 cup worth zucchini spirals
- 1/1 tbsp hemp or chia seeds
- 1 tbsp pine nuts
- 1 tablespoon Greek seasoning
- ½ low fat plain Greek yogurt

**Directions:**

In pot, mix together potatoes, cherry tomatoes, spirals, chia or hemp seeds, pine nuts Greek seasoning, and yogurt.

Cook on high pressure 5 minutes.

*QPR*

# Greek Mushrooms and Stewed Tomatoes

Cannot find cremini mushrooms? White button mushrooms make a great substitute! Makes 4 servings

**Ingredients:**

- 1 tbsp olive oil
- 2 diced shallots
- 2 cloves garlic, chopped
- ½ tbsp balsamic vinegar
- 1/2 teaspoons pepper
- ½ pound cremini mushrooms, sliced
- 1 tbsp olive
- 1 large can stewed tomatoes
- 1 teaspoon lemon zest
- 1 teaspoon black pepper
- 1 tablespoon Greek seasoning for a minty flavor, or herbs de Provence for a savory flavor
- ½ teaspoon Worchester sauce

**Directions:**

In large pot, over med-high heat combine olive oil, stewed tomatoes, lemon zest, black pepper, and seasoning or herbs. Bring to a boil, reduce heat, and simmer 25-30 minutes.

Preheat oven to 350F and prepare a casserole dish.

In a large bowl, whisk together onions, garlic, balsamic vinegar, pepper, herbs de Provence, and mushrooms.

Spread evenly in casserole dish , top with stewed tomatoes, and bake 30 minutes.

# Honey Garlic Potatoes & Peppers

Try it with jalapenos or jalapeno powder! Makes 4 servings

**Ingredients:**

- 2 garlic cloves, sliced
- 2 tsp smoked paprika
- 1 tsp diced parsley
- 4 tablespoons organic honey
- 3 tbsp olive oil
- ½ lbs. potatoes, sliced
- 1 shallot, sliced
- Juice of 1 lemon
- 1 tablespoon olive oil
- 1/2 tablespoon balsamic vinegar
- 1 teaspoon garlic, minced
- 1 onion cut into strips
- ½ tablespoon lemon zest
- 1 tablespoon rosemary, finely cut
- 2 bell peppers, rinsed, cored, and coarsely chopped

**Directions:**

Preheat oven to 425F and prepare 11x9 casserole dish.

In bowl, mix together olive oil, vinegar, garlic, onion, rosemary, and pepper pieces; cover and sit in refrigerator 20 minutes.

Mix together the minced garlic, paprika, honey, olive oil, potatoes, shallot; cover and let sit in refrigerator 20-30 minutes

In dish, spread potato mix and top with bell pepper mix.

Bake 40-45 minutes.

# Baked Vegetarian Chili

Great on cold nights! Makes 4 servings

**Ingredients:**

- 2 Tbsp olive oil
- 1/2 cup chopped red onion
- 1 teaspoon garlic, minced
- 1-piece turmeric, diced
- ½ tbsp diced oregano
- 1 8 oz. can diced tomatoes and green chilies
- 1 small can stewed or crushed tomatoes
- 1 tbsp tomato paste
- 2 cups low vegetable broth
- 1 pack meatless ground beef crumble
- 2 cups dark red kidney beans, drained and rinsed
- 20 crushed corn chips

**Directions:**

Preheat oven to 350F and prepare 9x9 dish.

Heat oil in a large pot over medium high heat.

Add onion, garlic, turmeric and sauté 3 minutes.

Add tomatoes, paste, broth, crumble, beans.

Bring to a boil then remove from heat.

Spread evenly into dish, top with crushed corn chips, and bake 30-35 minutes.

# Kale and Artichoke Linguine Casserole

Add some lemon peel and sweet ginger! Makes 4 servings

**Ingredients:**

- 1 tbsp extra virgin olive oil
- 4 oz. linguine, prepared
- 3 Campari tomatoes, quartered
- ½ cup matchstick carrots
- 1 diced shallot
- 2 cups artichokes, chopped
- 1 teaspoon garlic, minced
- 1 ½ cups water
- ½ teaspoon thyme
- ½ teaspoon oregano, chopped
- 1 teaspoon lemon juice
- Shredded mozzarella or parmesan cheese for top

**Directions:**

In pot, combine oil, tomatoes, carrots, artichokes, shallot, garlic, water.

Toss in cooked linguine, thyme, oregano, lemon juice.

Cook on high pressure 4 minutes.

*QPR*

# Turmeric Casserole

Try various paprikas and salsa spices! Makes 4 servings

**Ingredients:**

- ½ cup turmeric rice
- 1 cans chickpeas, drained and rinsed
- 6 cherry tomatoes, quartered
- ½ cup English cucumber, seeded and chopped
- 1 8 oz. can diced tomatoes and green chilies
- 1/2 red onion, diced
- 2/3 cup sliced Kalamata olives
- 1 tablespoons capers
- 1/3 cup lemon juice
- 1 teaspoon thyme
- 1 teaspoon diced basil
- 1 teaspoon diced parsley
- 1 cup water

**Directions:**

Preheat oven to 350F and prepare 9x9 dish

In a large bowl, combine rice, chickpeas, tomatoes, cucumbers, red pepper, olives, capers, lemon juice, thyme, basil, parsley, water.

Spread evenly into dish and bake 30 minutes.

# Cucumber & Asparagus Casserole

Add in fresh herbs an eggplant spirals! Makes 4 servings.

**Ingredients:**

- ½-pound asparagus, cut into 2-inch pieces
- 1 seedless cucumber sliced
- 2 Roma tomatoes sliced
- 1 can celery condensed cream of soup
- 1 tbsp e.v. olive oil
- 1/2 tablespoons lemon juice
- 1/2 teaspoons grated lemon zest
- 1/3 tsp thyme
- ½ tsp diced basil

**Directions:**

In pot, combine asparagus, cucumber, tomatoes, celery condensed soup, olive oil, lemon juice, lemon zest, thyme,

Cook on high 5 minutes.

*QPR*

# Shirataki Noodles

For extra flavor, add 1 tsp veg. bouillon paste (such as Better Then Bouillon) Makes 2 servings.

**Ingredients:**

- 1/4 cup diced onions
- 1 teaspoon minced garlic
- 1.2 tsp red pepper flakes or chili oil
- 1/3 tsp ground ginger
- 1/2 teaspoon pepper
- 1/3 cup diced tomatoes
- 1/3 cup diced eggplant
- 1/2 cup edamame or snow peas
- ½ cup matchstick carrots
- 4 cups organic vegetable broth
- 1/3 cup shirataki noodles
- 1 can cream of condensed mushroom soup

**Directions:**

In pot, mix onions, garlic, flakes or oil, ginger, pepper, tomatoes, eggplant, edamame, matchstick carrots, vegetable broth, noodles, condensed soup.

Cook on high heat 4-5 minutes.

*QPR*

# Instant Pot Yogurt Casserole

For some zing, add ½ tbsp onion seasoning like Lipton's packets! Makes 1 serving.

**Ingredients:**

- ½ cup jasmine rice kernels
- 1 cup plain Greek yogurt
- ½ tbsp flax seed
- ½ tsp lemon peel
- 1 sliced red onion
- 1 tsp garlic, minced
- 1 small can peas and carrots
- 1/2 cup garbanzo beans, washed
- ¼ cup plain breadcrumbs
- 2 teaspoon grated parmesan cheese
- 1 cup + 1 tbsp veg. stock or water

**Directions:**

Mix together rice kernels, yogurt, flax seed, lemon peel, red onion, minced garlic, peas and carrots, beans, breadcrumbs, cheese, liquid.

Spread evenly into dish.

Bake 30 minutes.

# Sesame Noodle Casserole

For added protein, add chickpeas! Makes 2 servings.

**Ingredients:**

- 1/2 teaspoon sesame oil
- ½ tablespoon coconut oil
- 2-4 drops chili oil
- 2 stems bok choy, washed and sliced (optional)
- ½ teaspoon garlic, minced
- ½ tsp red pepper flakes or paste
- 1/4 cup mirepoix
- 1 cup tofu, cubed
- 1/2 cup edamame
- 1 cup veggie stock (water works too)
- 1/2 cup worth rice noodles, uncooked

**Directions:**

In pot, combine sesame oil, coconut oil, chili oil, bok choy, minced garlic, red pepper flakes, mirepoix and sauté 1 minute.

Add in cubed tofu, edamame, stock or water, uncooked rice noodles. Stir well.

Cook on high pressure 4 minutes

*QPR*

## I.P Cantaloupe & Cucumber Bake

Use seasonal melons and fruits! Makes 2 servings.

**Ingredients:**

- 2 cups of cantaloupe
- 1 cup cubed butternut squash
- 1/2 seedless cucumber, sliced
- 1 can garbanzo beans, washed and drained
- ½ tbsp chia seeds
- 1/3 cup julienned red bell pepper
- ¼ teaspoon rice vinegar
- 1/3 cup olive oil
- ½ tbsp thyme
- 1 diced scallion
- 1 cup plain Greek yogurt
- 1 cup water

**Directions:**

In pot, combine cantaloupe chunks, butternut squash, cucumber slices, garbanzo beans, chia seeds, red pepper, rice vinegar, olive oil, thyme, Greek yogurt, water.

Cook on high pressure 5 minutes.

*QPR*

# Cauliflower Gnocchi Casserole

Serve with wine and crunchy bread! Makes 2 servings.

**Ingredients:**

- Olive oil for drizzling
- ¾ cup low fat coconut milk
- 1 cup cauliflower, florets
- 1 cup broccoli, florets
- 1/3 tbsp cassava flour
- 1 1/2 tsp tapioca flour
- ½ teaspoon thyme
- 3/4 teaspoon garlic, minced
- ½ teaspoon lemon peel
- 2 cups shredded cabbage

**Directions:**

Steam cauliflower & broccoli heads 5-7 minutes, ring out water, and then put in blender along with smoked paprika and cassava flour.

Blend till mix is smooth.

Cut each segment into 1-inch pieces, drop them into boiling water and let rise to surface.

In pot, whisk together coconut milk, pepper, lemon peel, minced garlic, tapioca flour. Stirring continuously until smooth and thickens.

Place cauliflower, broccoli, and cabbage shreds in pot and coat well with sauce.

Let simmer 5 minutes then spread evenly into dish.

Bake for 30 minutes.

# Sriracha Thyme Casserole

Throw some bell peppers or jalapenos in! Makes 2 servings.

**Ingredients:**

- 1/2 tablespoon butter or ghee
- 1/3 tbsp onion, grated
- 1/2 teaspoon garlic, minced
- 1 cup sweet potato spirals
- 1 burger crumble
- 1/4 cup coconut milk
- ½ tbsp tomato paste
- ½ tsp sriracha
- 1 1/2 teaspoons tapioca flour
- 1/4 teaspoons thyme, diced
- 1/3 teaspoon rosemary
- 1/4 teaspoon red pepper flakes

**Directions:**

Mix sweet potato spirals, flour, oil together.

In pot, melt butter and add julienned onions then sauté 1 minute.

Whisk in spirals, garlic, coconut milk, stir for 30 seconds.

Whisk in diced oregano, diced rosemary, tapioca flour, red pepper flakes.

Cook on high 30-45 minutes.

# Cayenne Casserole

Also great in the slow cooker! Makes 2 servings.

**Ingredients:**

- 2 large chopped carrots
- 1 chopped Roma tomato
- ¼ cup peas
- ¼ cup green beans
- 1 teaspoon Worcestershire sauce
- ½ teaspoon cayenne powder
- 1 cup parsley leaves
- 3-4 cups mushrooms
- 1 cup vegetable stock or water

**Directions:**

In pot, combine chopped carrots, chopped tomato, peas, green beans, Worcestershire sauce, cayenne powder, parsley, mushrooms, stock.

Cook on high pressure 5 minutes.

*QPR*

# Rice Noodle Bake

Try various noodles! Makes 2 servings.

**Ingredients:**

- 1 tbsp olive oil
- ¼ tsp chili oil or paste
- 1/3 tsp turmeric
- 1/3 tsp ground ginger
- ½ tbsp thyme
- 1 diced scallion
- 1/2 cup ground beef crumble
- 1/2 cup broken rice noodles
- 1/3 cup julienned green chili pepper
- ½ cup worth seaweed
- ½ cup water or veg. stock

**Directions:**

Mix olive oil, vinegar, and diced scallions.

Cover and chill at least ten minutes in fridge.

In pot, combine browned ground beef, kale, spirals, red bell pepper, stock.

Cook on high pressure 7 minutes.

*QPR*

# Kale & Carrots Casserole

Sub spinach for the kale! Makes 4 servings.

**Ingredients:**

- 1/3 cup shredded carrots
- ½ tsp pepper
- ½ teaspoon kale, finely chopped
- 1 teaspoon onion, minced or grated
- 1/2 tablespoon ginger, minced or grated
- 1/2 teaspoon brown sugar
- 1 egg, beaten
- 1 tbsp breadcrumbs (store bought or homemade)
- 1 cup water

**Directions:**

Mix mash, shredded carrots, pepper, kale, minced onion, minced ginger, brown sugar, beaten egg, breadcrumbs.

Spread evenly into dish.

Bake 30 minutes.

# Quick & Easy I.P Veggie Curry

Also great with a tahini sauce! Makes 2 servings.

**Ingredients:**

- 1/2 cups broccoli trees
- 1/3 cup plum tomatoes, quartered
- 1 clove garlic, chopped
- ¼ cup julienned caramelized onions
- 1 ½ cans full fat coconut milk
- 2 tablespoons curry sauce
- 1 tbsp parsley, chopped
- ½ tbsp chopped Italian oregano

**Directions:**

In pot, combine broccoli, tomatoes, garlic, onions, coconut milk withhold the cream, parsley, oregano.

Cook 7-8 minutes on manual.

Using a strainer remove veggies.

Add in milk cream.

Sauté 8-10 minutes until sauce reaches desired thickness.

Return veggies, mix well, serve over rice!

# Sweet Vegetable Curry

Use red or green curry powder! Makes 2 servings.

**Ingredients:**

- 2 cups cauliflower rice
- 1/2 tablespoons curry powder
- 1 teaspoon diced turmeric
- 1 burger crumble
- ½ tub cubed tofu
- 1/3 cup fire roasted diced tomatoes
- ½ tsp sweet ginger
- 1/2 teaspoon black pepper
- 1 1/2 cans full fat coconut milk
- 1 tablespoon coconut oil

**Directions:**

To pot add cauliflower rice, curry powder, turmeric, tomatoes, sweet ginger, black pepper, coconut milk no cream.

Cook 7-9 minutes on high pressure.

Stir coconut cream and oil into curry.

Sauté 5-7 minutes or until reduces and thickens.

*QPR*

# Spicy Cabbage Casserole

Add in ramen or soba noodles! Makes 2 servings.

**Ingredients:**

- ½ cup shredded cabbage
- 1/3 cup scallions, chopped
- 4-6 parsley leaves
- 1 tbsp diced olives
- 1 tbsp sliced mushrooms
- 1/2 teaspoon Italian oregano
- 1/2 teaspoon minced garlic
- ½ tsp sweet paprika
- ½ tsp red pepper flakes
- 1/3 tsp pepper
- 1/3 tsp cayenne pepper
- 1 dash Worchester sauce
- ¼ tsp cumin
- ¼ tsp onion powder
- 1 cup veg. stock or water

**Directions:**

Preheat oven to 350F and prepare 9x9 dish.

In bowl, combine cabbage, scallions, parsley, olives, mushrooms, oregano, garlic, paprika, red pepper flakes, pepper, cayenne pepper, Worchester sauce, cumin, onion powder, stock.

Spread evenly in dish.

Bake 30 minutes.

# Apple Pie French Toast Instant Pot Casserole

Add in extra cinnamon! Makes 2 serving.

**Ingredients:**

- 1 ½-2 cups white bread, cubed
- 1/2 teaspoon apple pie spice
- 2 eggs
- 1/3 cup unsweetened almond milk
- ½ tbsp bread and butter extract
- ½ tablespoon vegetable oil
- ½ tsp cinnamon
- ¼ tsp cloves

**Directions:**

Preheat oven to 350F and prepare 9x9 dish.

Mix apple pie spice, unsweetened almond milk, eggs, extract.

Spread bread cubes evenly across dish.

Pour milk mixture over cubes.

Bake 30 minutes.

# Peppers with Mushrooms, Avocado and Eggs

Great use for garden fresh peppers! Makes 2 servings.

**Ingredients:**

- 4 eggs
- 1/3 cup diced mushrooms
- 1 tsp cinnamon
- 1/3 cup diced avocado
- 2 red peppers
- 1 teaspoon oregano, diced
- 1 teaspoon rosemary, diced
- ¾ cup water
- ½ cup shredded cheddar cheese

**Directions:**

Preheat oven to 350F and prepare 9x9 dish

In a bowl, mix together eggs, diced mushrooms, and cinnamon.

Pour into dish.

Top with diced avocado, diced red bell peppers, diced oregano, diced rosemary, water, cheese.

Bake 30 minutes.

# Eggplant & Pumpkin Puttanesca

Delicious! Makes 2 serving

**Ingredients:**

- 1 tablespoon e.v olive oil
- 1/4 cup grated onion
- ½ tbsp garlic, minced
- ½ cup diced eggplant
- 1/3 cup diced pumpkin
- 1/3 cup tomato sauce
- 1 tablespoon tomato paste
- 1 tablespoon capers, drained
- 1 teaspoon red pepper flakes
- 1 cup keto linguine or fettucine
- 1-2 tsp. Italian seasoning
- ½ cup shredded Parmigiano-Reggiano for topping
- 1 cup veg. stock or water

**Directions:**

In pot, sauté olive oil, onions, and garlic 1-2 minutes.

Pour noodles in pot.

Place on top of noodles eggplant, pumpkin, tomato sauce, paste, capers, red pepper flakes, pasta, Italian seasoning.

Pour stock in middle.

Cook 8 minutes.

*QPR*

# Author's Afterthoughts

Thanks ever so much to each of my cherished readers for investing the time to read this book!

I know you could have picked from many other books, but you chose this one. So, a big thanks for reading all the way to the end. If you enjoyed this book or received value from it, I'd like to ask you for a favor. Please take a few minutes to **post an honest and heartfelt review on** *Amazon.com*. Your support does make a difference and helps to benefit other people.

*Thanks!*

**Julia Chiles**

Made in the USA
Coppell, TX
10 October 2023

22663063R00063